A HISTORICAL ALBUM OF
GEORGIA

A HISTORICAL ALBUM OF

GEORGIA

Charles A. Wills

THE MILLBROOK PRESS, Brookfield, Connecticut

Front and back cover: "Georgia Swamp." Unknown artist. Courtesy of Media Projects Incorporated Archives.

Title page: Confederate Generals of Stone Mountain. Courtesy of Stone Mountain Memorial Association.

Library of Congress Cataloging-in-Publication Data

Wills, Charles.
    A historical album of Georgia / Charles A. Wills.
       p.   cm. — (Historical albums)
    Includes bibliographical references (p. 62) and index.
    ISBN 0-7613-0035-X (lib. bdg.)   ISBN 0-7613-0125-9 (pbk.)
    1. Georgia—History—Juvenile literature. 2. Georgia—
Gazetteers—Juvenile literature. I. Title. II. Series.
F286.3.W53 1996
975.8—dc20
                                     96-16374
                                      CIP
                                      AC

 Created in association with Media Projects Incorporated

    C. Carter Smith, *Executive Editor*
    Douglas Hill, *Project Editor*
    Charles A. Wills, *Principal Writer*
    Bernard Schleifer, *Art Director*
    Christina Hamme, *Production Editor*
    Arlene Goldberg, *Cartographer*

    Consultant: W. Claybrook Cushman, Holy Innocents Episcopal School,
Atlanta, Georgia

Manufactured in the United States of America

10 9 8 7 6 5 4 3 2 1

CONTENTS

Introduction

In November 1864, the city of Atlanta, Georgia, was little more than charred ruins. Pounded by Union general William Sherman's artillery, abandoned by almost all its residents, and finally set afire, only a handful of its 1,200 original buildings remained standing.

When Atlanta's leading citizens gathered to plan the city's rebuilding, they chose the phoenix—a mythical bird that rises, reborn, from its own ashes—as a symbol for the revitalized city. It was a fitting choice. Within a few years, the city was not only rebuilt, it was bigger and more populous than it had been before the Civil War. The phoenix is a good symbol not just for Atlanta but for Georgia as a whole. Throughout its history, the state has suffered many setbacks—devastation in the Revolutionary and Civil wars, economic crises, social upheavals—but it has always recovered and gone on to greater things.

Georgia's amazing ability to create a better future from the ashes of the past is a testimony to the spirit of its people. The state's people, in turn, can draw on a rich and unique history for inspiration. This book is the story of that heritage. It is also the story of the many great people who helped make Georgia the dynamic place it is today—from the Native American chief Tomochichi to the humanitarian general James Oglethorpe, from the educator Martha McChesney Berry to the great civil rights leader Martin Luther King, Jr.

PART ONE

THE OLD SOUTH

Two field hands stand holding their cotton harvest in this 19th-century painting. In Georgia, cotton was the primary source of wealth for many generations.

The mountains, valleys, and coastal lowlands of Georgia were home to two powerful Native American nations—the Creeks and the Cherokees—when the first Europeans arrived in the 16th century. The region was ruled for years by the Spanish. Then, in 1733, Britain founded the colony of Georgia—the last of the original thirteen colonies. Established by General James Oglethorpe as a haven for debtors and religious refugees, Georgia grew slowly until after the Revolutionary War. In the first half of the 19th century, Georgia's economy became dependent on cotton produced by slaves, and when the Civil War began, Georgia threw in its lot with the Confederacy.

The Native Americans of Georgia

The Cherokees, a Native American people who lived in what is now Georgia, believed that a vast sea once covered their homeland. At the beginning of the world, they believed, a great bird had flown down from the sky and scooped up mud from the sea floor to create the land. When the great bird returned to the sky, its flapping wings shaped the mud into Georgia's hills and valleys.

In fact, an ocean did cover much of North America millions of years ago. Over time, the waters retreated, leaving the three distinctive regions that make up the state of Georgia.

In the north are the Blue Ridge Mountains, a link in the great Appalachian Mountain range that stretches from Georgia to Maine. In central Georgia, the mountains give way to the Piedmont Plateau—a region of rolling hills and low ridges. The third region, separated from the Piedmont Plateau by a range of hills called the Fall Belt, is the mostly flat coastal lowland, where Georgia meets the Atlantic Ocean. Besides these three mainland regions, Georgia also includes a string of beautiful offshore islands—the "Golden Isles."

People have lived in Georgia for about 10,000 years. Historians believe that prehistoric Georgia was part of a Mound Builder culture that flourished for thousands of years in the Southeast and Midwest. The remains of some mounds, probably built for religious purposes, have been found in the state. Almost 500 years ago, however, the Mound Builder culture mysteriously faded away.

Later, Native Americans from other regions arrived in Georgia. Over time, they developed into two distinct nations. The Cherokees, whose territory extended into Virginia and the Carolinas, lived in hilly northern Georgia. In the south was a loosely organized collection of tribes that European explorers later named the Creeks.

Although they spoke different languages and had some cultural differences, the Cherokees and Creeks shared a similar way of life. They lived in villages (some of which housed hundreds of people), where they farmed crops of corn, squash, beans, and tobacco. They also hunted and fished in Georgia's forests, rivers, and streams. Cherokees and Creeks occasionally went to war, but mostly they settled their disputes peacefully— sometimes by competing at *chunkee,* a lacrosse-like game.

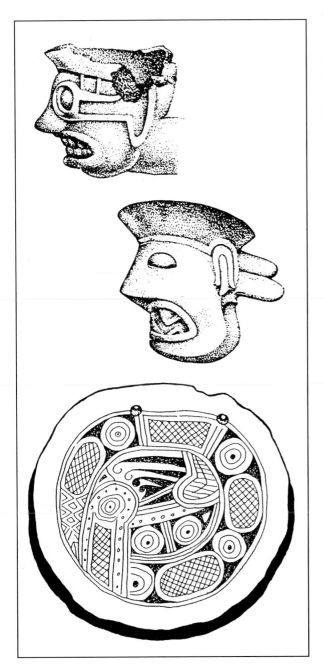

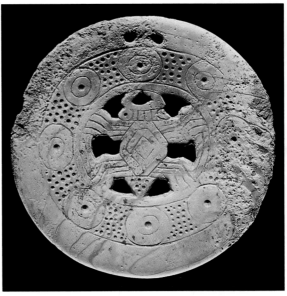

This shell (above), an artifact of the Mound Builder culture that spread across Georgia about 3,000 years ago, is engraved with a design that is thought to represent the sun. The two holes at the top probably mean that it was worn as a necklace.

These tobacco pipes (upper left) and engraved shell (lower left) also date back to the Mound Builder culture. Their designs closely resemble those found in ancient civilizations in present-day Mexico. Some historians believe that the Mound Builders traded with people as far away as Central America.

European Contact and International Conflict

For several hundred years, the Cherokees and Creeks had the hills and valleys of Georgia to themselves. Then, in the mid-1500s, a new and very different group of people arrived in the region.

It's not surprising that the first Europeans to reach Georgia came flying the red-and-gold flag of the Kingdom of Spain. After 1492, when Christopher Columbus (an Italian captain sailing in the Spanish king's service) reached the Caribbean in what Europeans called the New World, Spain took the lead in exploring and colonizing the Americas and the Caribbean islands.

Spanish ships touched the Georgia coast in the early 1500s, but it wasn't until 1540 that the first Spanish expedition made its way into the heart of Georgia. That year, a long procession of soldiers, priests, and Native American slaves led by the explorer Hernando de Soto crossed into Georgia from Florida.

The expedition spent about four months marching north and west across Georgia. The Creeks, who placed a high value on hospitality, greeted the Spanish with gifts. De Soto's soldiers repaid these gestures of friendship by clapping many Creeks

in chains and taking them along as slaves. (A century and a half later, the Creeks took revenge by destroying some of the early Spanish settlements in Georgia.) Before long, Spain claimed Georgia as part of Florida, calling the region Guale after an important Creek chief.

The next nation to take an interest in Georgia was France. The French attempted to plant a colony on the Georgia coast, but the effort ended in

disaster in 1564: Spanish troops
wiped out the settlers. Two years
later, to keep the French out of
Georgia, the Spanish built a fort on
St. Catherines Island. From this offshore outpost, Spanish priests set out
to establish missions, or religious settlements, as part of their effort to
convert the region's Native Americans
to Christianity. These missions were
the first European settlements on the
Georgia mainland.

This 19th-century painting by
Frederic Remington shows soldiers
of Hernando de Soto's *entrada*
(expedition) crossing a swamp. De
Soto died near the Mississippi
River in 1542, three years after
the expedition passed through
Georgia.

General Oglethorpe's Paradise

From the mid-1500s through the early 1700s, only a handful of Europeans lived in Georgia: the soldiers on St. Catherines Island, the priests in the missions, and a few adventurers and traders.

Elsewhere in North America in these years, France colonized Canada and explored the Mississippi Valley while England—a latecomer to North America—planted a string of colonies on the Atlantic coast to the north of Spanish Florida. Eager to drive the Spanish from the region, English colonists in the Carolinas supplied guns to Georgia's Creeks. The Creeks fought the Spanish so successfully that by the early 1800s the Spanish had abandoned their outposts in Georgia.

The Creeks then turned on their former allies, the English, invading South Carolina in 1715. The English colonists managed to beat back the Creeks, but South Carolina's narrow escape led many colonists and Britons to call for settlement of the land between the Carolinas and Florida.

Fifteen years later, a remarkable Englishman named James Oglethorpe proposed just such a colony. Oglethorpe's plan, however, was inspired more by his humanitarian beliefs than by Britain's desire to claim more of North America or to keep the Spanish isolated in Florida.

Born into a wealthy family in 1696, Oglethorpe first made a name for himself as a soldier. Then, still in his twenties, he left the military for a career in politics. He entered Parliament, England's legislature, where he won a reputation as a reformer by campaigning against slavery and impressment—the practice of taking men against their will and putting them in the Royal Navy.

Oglethorpe also opposed imprisonment for debt. In 18th-century Britain, if someone could not repay a

This engraving shows General James Oglethorpe as a young military man. Oglethorpe's able leadership earned him the admiration of colonists and Native Americans alike, as did his great generosity and kindness.

loan or other debt, he or she could be thrown into prison. Debtors' prisons were filthy, crowded hellholes in which many prisoners died of hunger and disease. Such was the fate of one of Oglethorpe's best friends, an architect named Robert Castell. Saddened by Castell's death, Oglethorpe and others began to work to improve conditions in debtors' prisons. They made progress but came up against the major flaw in the system: Once in prison, a debtor had no way of repaying his debts.

The solution, Oglethorpe believed, was to found an American colony where England's debtors (and other "deserving poor") could settle and work off their debts by producing goods for export to England. Oglethorpe also saw his proposed colony as a refuge for Europeans suffering religious persecution.

Oglethorpe presented his plan to King George II, who quickly realized that such a colony would also serve as a buffer against the Spanish to the south. In 1732, the king granted Oglethorpe and his associates a charter (royal permission) to settle the land between Florida and the Carolinas, and Oglethorpe pledged to name the colony Georgia in honor of his royal benefactor.

In November 1732, Oglethorpe and about 120 colonists left London aboard the galley *Anne*. Most of these original settlers were poor people lured by Oglethorpe's promise of fifty

The Yamacraw *mico* (chief) Tomochichi posed for this portrait on his journey to Britain in 1734. The young boy is his nephew and adopted son, Tooanahowi.

acres of land per family. The *Anne* landed in South Carolina early in 1733. Traveling ahead of the main party, Oglethorpe and a few others selected a site for the new colony's main settlement—a patch of high ground twenty miles upstream from the mouth of the Savannah River. It was called Yamacraw Bluff after the Native Americans who lived there.

The Yamacraws had split off from the Creek tribe many years before. Their *mico*, or chief, was Tomochichi,

These colonists are felling trees to build houses in the newly founded town of Savannah atop Yamacraw Bluff. This engraving appeared on a document printed by Georgia's trustees as part of a campaign to raise money for the colony.

a wise and able leader about eighty years old. With Mary Musgrove, the half-Creek, half-English wife of an English trader, acting as interpreter, Oglethorpe and Tomochichi pledged peace and friendship. In May 1733, Oglethorpe signed a formal treaty with fifty chiefs of the Lower Creek Nation. In return for massive land grants, the Creeks were given protection under British law and liberal trading rights.

Unlike most such agreements between settlers and Native Americans, this one lasted. Both peoples managed to get along. (Later, Tomochichi even traveled to England to meet the king; he died in Georgia and was then buried, at his own request, in the city of Savannah.)

The main group of English settlers arrived at Yamacraw Bluff from South Carolina on February 12, 1733. A town had already been laid out by architect William Bull, and the colonists set to work cutting down trees to build houses and planting crops in the new settlement they named Savannah, like the river beneath Yamacraw Bluff. During that first year, forty clapboard houses with log foundations rose along the shores of the river. A jail soon followed, and a government of courts and magistrates was organized. General Oglethorpe's "noble experiment," as many in Europe and North America had started calling it, had begun.

Soldiers, Settlers, and Slaves

The new colony never really served Oglethorpe's original purpose of providing a haven for debtors. Many new settlers arrived in the next few years, most of them religious refugees or poor people in search of a better life. The newcomers included people from Wales, Ireland, and Scotland, as well as England. They founded farms and a few settlements of their own. Scottish Highlanders, for example, established a town—New Inverness, now called Darien—on the Altamaha River in 1736.

The first Jews arrived in Savannah in 1734 and soon established a thriving community. Another large group of religious refugees were the Salzburgers—Lutherans who had been mistreated for their beliefs in mostly Catholic Austria. A year later, Oglethorpe returned from a trip to England with another group of German-speaking religious refugees, the peace-

The frontispiece of a 1732 account of the Salzburgers' journey from Austria to Georgia shows an emigrant couple carrying a Bible and the Augsburg Confession—a symbol of the Lutheran faith. The first Moravians, members of another German-speaking Protestant group, arrived in the colony a few years later.

loving Moravians. Together, these people—plus settlers from Italy, Switzerland, and other nations—made Georgia the most diverse of the thirteen English colonies on the Atlantic Coast.

Oglethorpe hoped to create a kind of ideal society in Georgia, but reality frustrated his dreams. His plans called for wine and silk to be the colony's chief exports. However, the grape vines and silkworms brought from Europe did not thrive in Georgia's soil. Most of the colonists wound up growing food crops. Georgia's most valuable exports in its early years were "naval stores" for Britain's warships—turpentine, pitch, and trees for masts.

Oglethorpe banned what he considered two great evils—alcohol and

Few colonial cities were planned as carefully as Savannah, shown here as it looked in 1734, the year after it was founded. William Bull, an architect brought from South Carolina by Oglethorpe, laid out the town based on a grid of straight streets, broken up by squares, parks, and a five-acre garden for each family.

slavery. However, traders from the Carolinas easily slipped into Georgia with casks of rum, and Georgians who wanted African-American slaves to work on their farms found ways around the ban on slavery. Some "rented" slaves from South Carolina planters for terms of 100 years. Oglethorpe's refusal to allow slavery was an enlightened policy for the time, but in some ways it slowed Georgia's growth. A settler might live better in Georgia than he could in England,

During the struggle against Spain from 1739–1743, Georgia was defended by both militia (local troops) and British army regulars. At left, wearing a kilt, is a private of the Highland Independent Company, a unit recruited from among Scottish settlers. At right is a sergeant of Britain's 42nd Regiment of Foot.

but without slaves he couldn't get rich the way many did in the other Southern colonies—by using slave labor to cultivate valuable crops like tobacco, rice, and indigo (a plant used for dyes). Thus, ambitious immigrants from England tended to settle in Virginia and the Carolinas, rather than Georgia.

For this reason, Georgia's population remained small in comparison with the other English colonies. A decade after its founding, Georgia had only a few thousand inhabitants, most of whom lived in and around Savannah. When colonists called on Oglethorpe to overturn the ban on slavery, the great humanitarian refused.

But if Oglethorpe was a humanitarian, he was also a soldier, and he had plenty of opportunities to use his military talents in Georgia's early years. Relations with the Spanish, always tense, flared into war in 1739. The following year, Oglethorpe led armed colonists and Creek warriors south in an attempt to capture St. Augustine, the main Spanish settlement in Florida. They were unsuccessful and, beset by disease, quickly returned to Georgia.

In 1742, a fleet of Spanish warships landed 3,000 soldiers on St. Simons

Island off the Georgia coast. The Spanish, who outnumbered Oglethorpe and his forces by more than four to one, were preparing to drive the English from the region. Oglethorpe called on every Georgian man who could carry a gun, plus his Native American allies, and together they faced the Spanish on July 7. When the Spanish soldiers made the mistake of stopping to rest in a low-lying swamp, Oglethorpe and his men ambushed them. So many Spanish troops were killed that the swamp ran red with blood, and the victory became known as the Battle of Bloody Marsh.

For a small fight in a remote corner of the world, the Battle of Bloody Marsh had a great impact. After the battle, the Spanish presence in North America was limited to Florida, California, and the Southwest. Despite his victory, however, Oglethorpe was called to Britain to answer charges that he had bungled the expedition and mismanaged Georgia's finances. Although he was cleared of the accusations, he never returned to Georgia. He died in 1785, honored as one of the most progressive leaders of the time.

With Oglethorpe gone, his "noble experiment" gradually ended. By 1750, Georgia's trustees—the group of Englishmen who ran the colony's government from overseas—overturned the ban on slavery. Two years later, Georgia's original charter was returned to the king, and Georgia became a royal colony under the direct rule of the British government.

This map shows St. Augustine, the chief settlement and fortress of Spanish Florida, and the position of the invasion force led by Oglethorpe in 1740. Disease struck down so many of the attackers, however, that Oglethorpe decided to abandon the attack, returning to Georgia after a campaign of only five weeks.

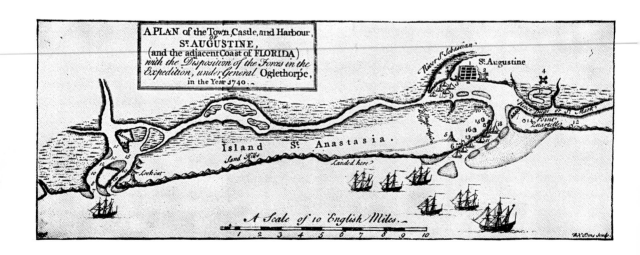

A PLAN of the Town, Castle, and Harbour, OF St AUGUSTINE, (and the adjacent Coast of FLORIDA) with the Disposition of the Forces in the Expedition, under General Oglethorpe, in the Year 1740.

A Scale of 10 English Miles.

A Colony Divided, A New State Born

The two decades following Georgia's transfer to the crown were a time of great growth. Savannah remained the colony's capital and chief city, while established towns grew and new communities were founded.

By the mid-1770s, Georgia's population had risen to about 40,000, about half of whom were African-American slaves working on the 1,400-odd plantations. These plantations were located mainly in the lowland area between the Savannah and Altamaha rivers, and their chief crop was rice. However, large plantations with many slaves were the exception. In upcountry, or inland, Georgia, it was more common to see small family farms with perhaps a slave or two.

In the 18th century, treaties with the Cherokees and Creeks opened up millions of inland acres to settlement. Ambitious newcomers from Britain,

At the end of the 18th and in the first decade of the 19th centuries, the Creeks and Cherokees agreed to sell almost all of their Georgia homelands. This proclamation (top) announces a treaty signed in March 1773, deeding large portions of tribal lands to the British.

In 1811, a council of Creek chiefs tried to stop the loss of their land by outlawing further sales, but some leaders, like William McIntosh (bottom), continued to sell the land. McIntosh paid for this disobedience with his life: He was killed by the Creek chief Menawa in 1825.

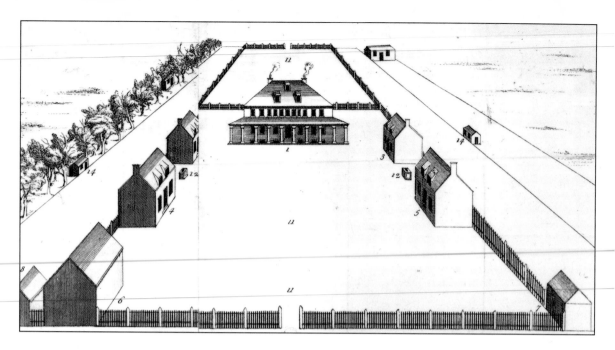

Virginia, and the Carolinas settled the upcountry region, where they grew food crops and grazed cattle for sale in Savannah and other towns. (The cracking sound of the cattle drovers' whips as they brought their cattle to market is the source of the term "Georgia cracker," a nickname given to upcountry people.)

With growth came culture, and Savannah's first public library opened in the early 1760s. The colony's first newspaper, the Georgia *Gazette,* began publication in 1763. Georgia lagged behind New England in the quality of its schools, but the colony boasted one fine educational institution—the Bethesda School in Bethesda, originally founded as an orphanage by the English missionary George Whitefield.

In the 1760s, relations between Britain and her thirteen colonies began to grow strained. Between 1754 and 1763, Britain and France had fought a great war for control of North America—the French and Indian War. Britain won, but the cost of victory led Parliament to introduce new taxes in the colonies. Many colonists resented the taxes because the colonies weren't represented in Parliament.

Especially hated was the Stamp Act of 1765, which taxed all kinds of paper goods. Georgia's Sons of

Liberty, a branch of a radical Patriot society active throughout the colonies, tried to stop a British tax agent from doing business in Georgia. They failed, but the incident angered many conservative Georgians who wanted to preserve good relations with Britain. Tensions eased for a time after Parliament repealed the Stamp Act, but new taxes and other laws enacted in the 1770s put Britain and the colonies on the road to conflict.

Opposition to British rule was lukewarm in Georgia. Last of the thirteen colonies to be founded, it still had many citizens of British birth, and its ties to the "mother country" were closer than those of other colonies. When colonial representatives met in Philadelphia in 1774 to form the First Continental Congress, Georgia did not even send delegates. But by early 1775, Georgia's Patriots were strong enough to mount a takeover of the colony's government. With their headquarters at Tondee's Tavern in Savannah, they organized a provincial

In November 1765, the Stamp Act caused colonists to voice angry protests. Its repeal three months later showed Georgians that there was power in unity among the colonies. In this British cartoon, the Stamp Act lies in a tiny coffin in the arms of a politician.

OR THE FUNERAL OF MISS AME-STAMP

congress and put the royal governor under house arrest.

The first shots of the Revolutionary War in Georgia were fired in March 1776—almost a year after the conflict began—when British warships sailed up the Savannah River to seize cargoes of rice. When the Second Continental Congress opened that summer, Georgia sent three delegates—Button Gwinnet, Lyman Hall, and George Walton. The three signed the Declaration of Independence, the document that created the United States of America and turned Georgia from a colony into a state.

This political victory was followed by a serious military defeat for Georgia's Patriots. As the year 1778 ended, British forces landed near Savannah and captured the port. In the upcountry region, Patriot forces managed to hold off British invaders for a time, but in 1779 the British gained control of most of the colony.

In October 1779, Major General Benjamin Lincoln of the Continental Army (the chief Patriot fighting force) led a campaign to retake Savannah. Despite help from the French navy (France had joined the war on the Patriot side), the attack proved a costly failure. More than 1,000 French and Patriot troops were killed or wounded—including Count Casimir Pulaski, a liberty-loving Polish nobleman fighting for the Patriot cause.

Finally, in 1781, the tide turned in the Patriots' favor. While Patriot and

A British bullet strikes Count Casimir Pulaski as he leads a cavalry charge during the bloody and unsuccessful attempt to retake Savannah on October 9, 1779. This Patriot defeat allowed the British to gain control of most of Georgia and South Carolina.

French forces trapped a British army at Yorktown in Virginia, Continental troops slowly recaptured most of Georgia from the British. The British surrender at Yorktown in October ended the major fighting and assured America's independence—but it was not until July 11, 1782, that British forces left Savannah and the stars and stripes of the new United States of America finally flew over the city.

Pioneers, Planters, and Displacement

Georgia suffered terribly during the Revolutionary War. Historians estimate that as much as half the property in the state was destroyed during the conflict. Damage was especially bad in the upcountry region, where Tories (colonists loyal to Britain) and Patriots had waged a vicious guerrilla conflict.

Yet the new state recovered quickly, thanks mostly to the availability of land on the frontier. Georgians who had fought for the Patriot cause were rewarded with large land grants, and there was plenty of acreage left over for people who wanted to try their luck at frontier farming. The lure of land in Georgia brought immigrants from other states and from overseas— so many that in 1790 Georgia's population was 82,000, more than double the figure at the start of the Revolutionary War.

Colonial boundaries were so vague that no one really knew how much land Georgia had. In 1795, dishonest investors bought 50 million acres of western land—land the state had no clear claim to—by bribing corrupt members of the state legislature. This Yazoo Land Fraud, as it came to be known, took years to sort out. Finally, in 1802, the state government turned the Yazoo land over to the federal government.

While hardy pioneer families pushed the Georgia frontier westward, the state's plantation economy got a boost from an unlikely source— a Connecticut Yankee named Eli Whitney. In 1793, Whitney visited Catherine Littlefield Greene, the widow of Revolutionary War general Nathanael Greene, at her plantation outside Savannah. Cotton was among the crops grown on Mrs. Greene's plantation. Small amounts of cotton had been grown in the South for decades, but it wasn't a very profitable crop because separating cotton seed from fiber was a long, hard process.

Although Eli Whitney (1765-1825) is best remembered for his invention of the cotton gin, he also built the first successful milling machine and devised several innovative manufacturing techniques, which had great impact on industrial development in the North.

Whitney's imagination was sparked by a suggestion from Mrs. Greene, and he set to work solving the problem. The result was the cotton gin (short for 'engine'), a simple machine that easily separated seed from fiber.

It wasn't long before the cotton gin transformed the economy of the South. Cotton became Georgia's major cash crop, and production increased twentyfold in just five years. But by making cotton planting profitable, the gin also tightened slavery's hold on Georgia and the other cotton-producing states of the South.

While the cotton economy began to flourish, Georgia's remaining Native Americans began a long ordeal that would end in tragedy.

Of Georgia's two main Native American groups, the Creeks had given up almost all their land before the Revolutionary War. What remained of their power was virtually

Slaves are shown here operating a cotton gin. Before the gin, it was a full day's work for one slave to remove the seeds from a single pound of cotton. After the gin's appearance, the same slave could process as much as fifty pounds of cotton per day.

destroyed in the War of 1812, in which many Creeks sided with the British.

On the other hand, thousands of Cherokees remained in Georgia—the only large group of Native Americans still living on their own land east of the Mississippi River. Unlike most Native American groups, the Cherokees had adapted well to the white way of life. In Georgia, they farmed successfully, built prosperous towns like their tribal capital, New Echota, and even developed a written version of their language.

Their success made them the target of jealous whites who wanted their fertile homeland. But it was lust for gold, not hunger for land, that set tragic events in motion for Georgia's Cherokees. In 1828, gold was found at Dahlonega, within the boundaries of the Cherokee Nation. Dahlonega and the surrounding area was quickly overrun by fortune hunters.

The Cherokees went to court to keep their land. Their case eventually reached the Supreme Court, which ruled in their favor—a rare legal victory for Native Americans, but an empty one. The Cherokees never saw the ruling enforced, because the federal government had already agreed to remove the Cherokees from Georgia as part of the Yazoo settlement two decades earlier.

Furthermore, the old Indian fighter Andrew Jackson was in the White House, and he favored the white

Sequoya (c. 1779–1843), the son of a British trader and a Cherokee woman, invented a written language for the Cherokees in 1821.

Georgians who wanted the Cherokees out of the state. "John Marshall has made his decision," President Jackson reportedly said, referring to the chief justice of the Supreme Court. "Now let him enforce it!"

So began one of the most tragic and shameful episodes in American history. In 1838, the U.S. Army arrived in Georgia to begin the forced removal of the Cherokees to a barren reservation in Indian Territory—the modern state of Oklahoma. About 15,000 people were herded west at bayonet point. Perhaps a quarter of the entire Cherokee population died during the difficult journey, which the survivors would remember bitterly as the Trail of Tears.

King Cotton

By 1820, Georgia's plantations were harvesting 90,000 bales (or 36 million pounds) of cotton each year. By 1860, that figure had escalated to 700,000 bales, but by then several other Southern states had passed Georgia in overall cotton production.

As in colonial times, there were few large plantations in Georgia, and only about 35 percent of white Georgians owned slaves. The census of 1860 found only 23 planters owning more than 200 slaves.

The image of life in Georgia popularized by the novel and movie *Gone With the Wind*—vast plantations, white-columned mansions, elegant dances—was enjoyed by only a few Georgians. Nevertheless, cotton was so important to the state that the small class of large-scale planters controlled the state government at Milledgeville, Georgia's capital.

The majority of white Georgians were independent farmers, and even people who worked in towns kept farms "on the side." Some prospered; others faced a daily struggle to grow enough food to feed their families, especially those living in the less-fertile hill country of northern Georgia.

Yet Georgia was a prosperous state. The huge expansion of Georgia's cotton economy would have been impossible without the people least able to enjoy it: African-American slaves. As more cotton was produced, Georgia's slave population grew, and by 1860 there were about 465,000 African-American slaves in Georgia. (The white population was 591,000.)

Life for Georgia's slaves varied widely from plantation to plantation. All worked hard. Some received decent treatment from their masters, while others endured miserable living conditions and cruel punishment.

Fear of slave uprisings led to harsh laws aimed at keeping slaves "in their place." In December 1829, for example, the state legislature made it a crime to teach African Americans to read or write. A few years later, another law forbade African Americans from doing business on their own.

Wealth from cotton did help advance education in Georgia, but

As in the rest of the South, Georgia's slaves combined West African and American influences to create a rich culture of their own. In this painting, a slave couple "jumps the broom"—a form of marriage ceremony. Rituals like this were necessary because many slave owners refused to recognize marriages between slaves.

only for a limited segment of the population. The state's first school of higher education, the University of Georgia at Athens, was founded shortly after the Revolutionary War. By 1860, Georgia had more than forty colleges—mostly small schools associated with various churches. Higher education was limited mostly to males, although one successful college for women, the Georgia Female College (later renamed Wesleyan College) did open in 1838.

It took Georgia decades to establish a statewide public school system. The state supported schools for the children of poor rural farmers, but these schools were often of poor quality. Children whose labor was needed on the family farm could come to school only occasionally. As a result, about a

fourth of Georgia's white adults couldn't read or write in the mid-1800s. In 1858, Governor Joseph Emerson Brown finally oversaw the creation of a true statewide public school system, but unfortunately the Civil War broke out before the system was in place.

The rise of the Cotton Kingdom also led to improvements in Georgia's transportation system. After 1820, steamboats were a common sight on the Savannah and Altamaha rivers, their decks piled high with bales of cotton. A decade later, the state's first railroad tracks were laid. By 1860, Georgia boasted some 1,200 miles of track—more than any Southern state. Most of these railroads ran from west to east, linking inland farms with the major coastal ports of Brunswick and

Savannah, or with Augusta on the Savannah River.

The most important railroad in pre–Civil War Georgia was the Western & Atlantic, which connected Chattanooga, Tennessee, to Savannah. The Western & Atlantic passed through a tiny backwoods village at a spot the Cherokees called Standing Peachtree. When the railroad first reached it, the village was renamed Terminus, then Marthasville (after the daughter of the Western & Atlantic's president).

In 1845, its name was changed again—to Atlanta. By then, several railroads used Atlanta as a junction, and within a decade the village grew into a thriving city of 10,000 people. Atlanta was on its way to becoming the transportation hub of the South.

Three machines—the cotton gin, the locomotive, and the steamboat—combined with the practice of slavery to create the Cotton Kingdom of pre–Civil War Georgia. At left, trainloads of cotton bales pass through a rail yard, perhaps on their way to Savannah for shipment to the mills of New England or Europe.

Slaves harvest cotton in this painting by William A. Walker (above). In the 1850s, an able-bodied male field hand sold for about $1,500 in Georgia's slave markets. Not all slaves worked in the field: Many were house servants, and those with special skills—nurses, and the like—were often hired out by their masters.

Georgia and the War Between the States

By the middle of the 19th century, the Northern and Southern states were approaching a crisis. The North, without slavery, was developing a powerful industrial economy fueled by the labor of thousands of immigrants from overseas. The South was less populous, less industrialized, less attractive to immigrants, and dependent on cotton and other cash crops. The slave system was needed to produce those crops.

At the time, most Northerners seemed content to leave slavery alone in the South—although a radical minority of Abolitionists (people who wanted to totally abolish slavery) loudly called for an end to the system. Many people in the North, however—even those who were not Abolitionists—didn't want slavery to spread into the new states and territories being created west of the Mississippi River. They also resented the power that the Southern legislators held in Congress.

For decades, political compromises had kept peace between the North and South, but the crisis finally came to a head in 1860. Abraham Lincoln, the candidate of the antislavery Republican Party, won the presidential election that year. Many Southern states were unwilling to accept the election results and began to secede (withdraw) from the Union. Senator Robert Augustus Toombs of Georgia, a fiery supporter of slavery and secession, declared that Georgia was "on the warpath!"

Although many white Georgians had no love for the planter class that

While serving in the House of Representatives, Georgian Alexander H. Stephens (1812–1883) joined with Northern congressmen to draft the Compromise of 1850, a set of laws that kept the peace between North and South for a time. When secession came, however, Stephens accepted the vice presidency of the Confederate States of America. Imprisoned for six months following the Confederacy's defeat, Stephens was elected governor of Georgia in 1883, but died shortly after taking office.

controlled the state government, there was plenty of enthusiasm for secession in the state. On January 19, 1861, a statewide convention voted by a wide margin to leave the Union. Soon afterward, Georgia joined the Confederate States of America—the new "nation" formed by the seceding Southern states. Alexander Stephens, a former Georgia congressman, was elected vice president of the Confederacy; Robert Augustus Toombs served for a time as the Confederate secretary of state, and later as a commander in the army.

When war broke out between the North and South in April 1861, young Georgian men crowded the

This painting captures only a little of the fury of the Battle of Chickamauga, one of the costliest combats of the war—for both sides. A Southern private who fought along Chickamauga Creek later described the noise of the battle as "one solid, unbroken wave of awe-inspiring sound, as if all the fires of earth and hell had been turned loose."

recruiting offices. About 125,000 Georgians served in the Confederate army, many thousands of whom lost their lives to disease or wounds.

Georgia soon proved its worth as an arsenal and storehouse of the Confederacy. While the state had little industry by Northern standards, it did have more factories and workshops than most other Confederate

Binoculars in hand, General William Tecumseh Sherman watches as a Union artillery battery sends shells crashing into Atlanta. Union fire claimed six civilian lives during the siege. Sherman's forced evacuation of the city, which later burned, made him a monster in the eyes of most Georgians.

states. These factories were soon turning out rifles, ammunition, cannons, and other supplies, which were rushed to the soldiers on the battlefield. Georgia's railroads made up a vital part of the Confederacy's transportation system.

The war stimulated production of farm products as well. Wartime restrictions on cotton planting caused farmers to produce alternative crops. Georgia's corn, wheat, sugar, and rice helped feed the army.

Joseph Brown, Georgia's governor from 1857 through the end of the war, skillfully managed the state's economy to provide the greatest amount of support for the Confederacy. Still, he often clashed with

Confederate president Jefferson Davis—for example, by keeping Georgia's troops from the Confederate army when he believed the state was in danger of invasion.

Invasion did come, but not until later in the war. The first important battle on Georgian soil came in April 1862, when Union warships landed troops and artillery on Tybee Island at the mouth of the Savannah River. Union cannons quickly pounded Fort

Pulaski—the main fortification protecting the port of Savannah—into rubble. This closed the vital port to ships and helped make the Union blockade of the Confederate coastline more effective.

In September 1863, 60,000 Union troops under Major General William Rosecrans advanced into northwest Georgia from recently captured Chattanooga, Tennessee. A Confederate force under Major General Braxton Bragg met them along the banks of a stream called Chickamauga Creek.

Chickamauga means River of Death in Cherokee—a name that turned out to be appropriate. In a furious two-day battle, 34,700 Union and Confederate soldiers were killed or wounded there. The Union force retreated into Chattanooga, but Bragg's casualties were so great that the battle was hardly a victory for the South.

In the spring of 1864, Brigadier General William Tecumseh Sherman—a name Georgians would pronounce with hatred for generations—marched a Union army into Georgia. Sherman's goal was to capture Atlanta and then to destroy as much of Georgia's war-making capability as he could.

Taking Atlanta was no easy task, thanks to the skillful defense mounted by Confederate general Joseph E. Johnston. Throughout the spring and into the summer, the two generals maneuvered around each other, Sherman attempting to encircle Atlanta,

and Johnston determined to stop him from doing so. When Sherman tried a direct attack on the Confederate positions at Kennesaw Mountain, his troops suffered a bloody setback.

Then the Confederate leadership replaced Johnston with the reckless John Bell Hood. In three pitched battles in the Atlanta suburbs—Peachtree Creek, Decatur, and Ezra Church— Sherman gained the upper hand. By August, Sherman had Atlanta surrounded and under heavy shelling. On September 2, Union troops entered the city, and the Confederacy lost its greatest inland city and transportation center.

Promoted to major general, Sherman led his army out of Atlanta in November. He was determined, as he told Union commander Ulysses S. Grant, to "make Georgia howl." The Union soldiers left behind a city in ruins. Fires, perhaps started by troops doing some last-minute looting, raged through Atlanta and practically leveled the city.

So began Sherman's famous March to the Sea. It saw little fighting—there were few troops left to defend Georgia—but much destruction. Followed by crowds of freed slaves and by bandits called "bummers," Sherman's army left a trail of devastation across central Georgia measuring fifty miles wide and stretching from Atlanta all the way to the Atlantic Ocean. Railroad tracks were torn up, farms and plantations burned, livestock slaughtered—anything of value to the Confederate war effort, and much that wasn't, was seized or destroyed. Sherman believed his actions were necessary and justified. Most white Georgians thought otherwise.

Sherman finally reached Savannah in late December. With supply lines destroyed and an army in ruins, the port fell quickly and was spared the destruction that Atlanta had witnessed. For all practical purposes, Georgia was now out of the war.

Five months later, Confederate commander Robert E. Lee surrendered at Appomattox Courthouse, Virginia, thus ending the Civil War. A month after that, Union cavalrymen captured Jefferson Davis near Irwinville, Georgia, as he attempted to flee overseas.

In an attempt to cut off the Confederates' supplies, Sherman ordered his army to destroy railway lines as they marched across the South. Here, the Nashville and Chattanooga depot in Atlanta lies in ruins.

GEORGIA REBORN

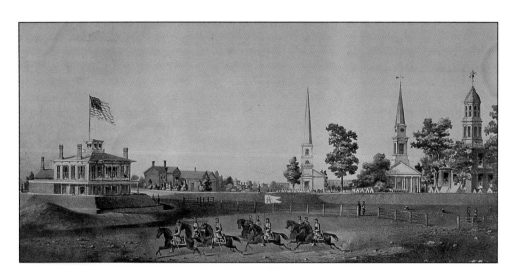

Following the Civil War, Georgians quickly rebuilt their cities. This square in Atlanta shows little evidence of the destruction that occurred elsewhere in the city only a few months earlier.

Georgia suffered greatly in the Civil War. With the beginnings of industrialization, its economy recovered in the 1870s. But the state remained mostly agricultural well into the 20th century, with many of its citizens—especially African Americans—trapped in a tenant-farming system known as sharecropping. World War II touched off decades of economic and population growth. At the same time, the state's African Americans struggled to achieve the civil and political rights they had long been denied. Today, Georgia—with its fast-growing capital, Atlanta—is among the most dynamic areas in the nation.

The New South

The Civil War left Georgia's economy in ruins and its society in turmoil. Historians estimate that Sherman's March to the Sea alone destroyed $100 million worth of property. The burning of Atlanta and other war damage throughout the state accounted for millions more.

Georgian men staggered home from the tattered remains of the Confederate armies and from Union prison camps, many of them finding their homes and farms destroyed. Hunger and disease stalked the state from the hills to the coast, preying on men, women, and children weakened by years of wartime hardship.

The state's African Americans struggled to survive and to come to terms with their new freedom. Some remained on the plantations where they had been slaves. Many became refugees in Georgia's cities, where they were helped by a federal agency called the Freedmen's Bureau.

What remained of Georgia's state government met at Milledgeville in October 1865. While the legislature acknowledged that slavery had been ended "by events," it refused to ratify (approve) the Fourteenth Amendment to the Constitution, which guaranteed basic civil rights to African Americans.

Georgia's failure to ratify the amendment caused Congress to set up a military government. With Union troops to protect them from vengeful whites, many freed slaves were able to vote, and they elected a legislature that included thirty-two African Americans. This "reconstructed" government, led by Governor Rufus Bullock, a Northerner, was hated by many white Georgians. Only the presence of federal troops—which some whites bitterly called "bayonet rule"—kept it in power.

Georgia was finally readmitted to the Union in 1870. By then the Northern public and the federal government had begun to lose interest in protecting the rights of African Americans in the South. African Americans were driven out of the Georgia legislature and out of politics altogether—a process abetted by the violent activities of the Ku Klux Klan and other white terrorist groups.

A decade after the Civil War, Georgia's African Americans found themselves in a condition not much different from slavery. Segregation (the forced separation of whites and African Americans on trains and in theaters, restaurants, and other public accommodations) became the law.

Many African Americans remained tied to the land through the sharecropping system. Under this system, African-American families (and many poor whites) farmed cotton or other crops on someone else's land. The sharecropper had to pay the landowner a large part of the crop as rent and

In this photograph (left), every member of a Georgian sharecropper family is picking cotton, even young children. In the decades after the Civil War, most sharecroppers lived under the "fifty-fifty" system. The sharecropper divided his crop fifty-fifty with the landlord, but he had to pay the landlord for tools, seed, and food.

The law was often of little help in protecting African Americans from violent, angry whites. "Southern Justice" (below), a picture series which ran in Harper's Weekly in the 1870s, depicts civil rights violations throughout the South, including white policemen beating African Americans on a Georgia street.

usually had to purchase seeds, food, and other necessities from the landowner—often at inflated prices. Sharecropping made it almost impossible for African Americans to own their own land or to save any money.

Together, segregation and sharecropping made Georgia's African Americans second-class citizens in their own state. The sharecropping system lasted well into the 20th century, and segregation didn't come to an end until the rise of the civil rights movement in the 1950s and 1960s. In some ways, though, Georgia made a quick and remarkable recovery from the ravages of the Civil War. This was certainly the case in Atlanta.

When Sherman marched out of the city, only 400 of Atlanta's 1,200 buildings remained standing. Rebuilding began immediately, and by late 1865, the city's population was double what it had been in 1860. By 1867, the railroads were running again, and Atlanta had again assumed its role as "crossroads of the South."

Atlanta's rebirth was fueled by the exploitation of the state's natural resources—especially timber and coal from the northern hills—and by the introduction of new industries like brick making and textiles. Already Georgia's economic capital, Atlanta became its political capital as well when the state legislature moved to Atlanta from Milledgeville in 1868.

Throughout the South, and especially in Georgia, farsighted people

Henry Grady (1850–1889) was editor of the Atlanta *Constitution* and a tireless promoter of the New South. Grady was only thirty-eight years old when he died of an illness caught during a speaking trip in the Northern states.

hoped for the rise of a prosperous New South from the ashes of war. The rapid, successful rebuilding of Atlanta came to symbolize this movement, which Atlanta *Constitution* editor Henry Grady summed up in a famous speech in 1886: "The Old South rested everything on slavery and agriculture.... The New South presents ... a hundred farms for every plantation... and a diversified industry that meets the complex needs of this complex age."

New Century, Old Problems

The promise of the New South was only partially fulfilled. Despite the industrialization of the 1870s and 80s, agriculture remained the mainstay of Georgia's economy. Cotton was still the chief crop, although large-scale fruit production—especially pecans and peaches—grew in importance.

Still, many of Georgia's small, independent farmers—those who farmed their own land as opposed to sharecropping—were unhappy with conditions as the 19th century ended. Before the Civil War, a small group of wealthy planters had dominated Georgia's government. The planter class faded into history in 1865, but after the war another small group of men, this time wealthy bankers and industrialists, came to control the state's economy and government.

Georgia's farmers felt these "Bourbons," as they were called (after the old royal family of France), taxed them unfairly and favored the interests of the railroads and factories over those of the farmer. The farmers soon found a champion in Thomas Watson.

A fiery speaker, Watson won election to Congress in 1890 and soon became a leading figure in the People's Party, a political organization that had a great following among farmers and small businesspeople in the Southern and Western states. (The movement was known as Populism.) In Washington, Watson oversaw the passage of the Rural Free Delivery Bill, which gave free mail delivery to people living far from towns and cities. Less than half of Georgia's 3 million people lived in towns or cities at the beginning of the 20th century.

A powerful writer and spellbinding speaker, Tom Watson (1856–1922) edited *The People's Party Paper* and later his own periodical, *Tom Watson's Magazine*. Early in his career Watson urged cooperation between Georgia's African Americans and whites. However, when few African Americans supported the Populist Party (partly from fear of white violence), he urged that they be barred from politics.

For Georgia's African Americans, who now made up about 40 percent of the population, life remained a struggle against poverty and prejudice. There were few educational opportunities, although two African-American colleges—Atlanta University and Morehouse College—opened soon after the Civil War.

The great African-American leader Booker T. Washington made a famous speech in Atlanta in 1895, urging African Americans to strive for equality through education and hard work. Yet many white Georgians fought any attempt by the state's African Americans to improve their lives, and racial conflict was never far beneath the surface of Georgia life.

In 1906, for example, Atlanta was swept by a four-day race riot that left ten African Americans and two white people dead. In rural Georgia, African

Booker T. Washington's famous speech at the 1895 Cotton States Exposition in Atlanta made him a leading spokesman for African Americans. Yet many disagreed with his belief that African Americans should stay out of politics and seek economic success as a first goal. Washington's major supporter in Georgia was Benjamin J. Davis, who founded an African-American newspaper, the Atlanta *Independent*, in 1903.

The tiny boll weevil moved north from Mexico in the early 1900s, devastating cotton crops throughout the South. In the long run, however, this destructive insect probably benefited Georgia's economy by making it less dependent on cotton and by forcing farmers to plant different crops, like peanuts and fruit.

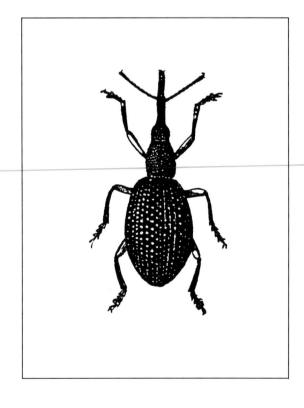

Americans were lynched (murdered by mobs) with terrible frequency. It is thought that about 500 African Americans were lynched in Georgia between 1890 and 1930.

Although Georgia's long-delayed public-school system finally began operating in 1871, it didn't reach all Georgian children, especially in the poor northern counties. To remedy this, educator Martha McChesney Berry used her own money to open schools in the region. The first Berry School opened in 1902.

Another Georgian woman, Juliette Gordon Low, influenced generations of American girls by founding the Girl Scouts of America in 1912.

America's entry into World War I in 1917 gave Georgia's economy a boost. Savannah became a major ship-building center, and factories in Atlanta, Macon, Augusta, and other cities turned out great quantities of war materials. (Atlanta suffered a serious fire in 1917, but, as in 1865, its citizens rebuilt with amazing speed.) Almost 100,000 Georgians served in the armed forces during the conflict.

After the war, a deadly invader moved into Georgia—the boll weevil. This small insect eats away at the boll, or fiber, of the cotton plant with devastating results. After ravaging cotton crops in Alabama, Mississippi, and other states, the weevil began to infest Georgia's cotton fields. Georgia and the other cotton-dependent Southern states went into a serious economic

In 1886, J.S. Pemberton mixed up the first batch of Coca-Cola in the back of his Atlanta drugstore. Pemberton later sold the secret formula to another pharmacist, Asa Griggs Candler, who set up a company to bottle and market the beverage. By the time this advertisement appeared in 1905, Coca-Cola was on its way to becoming the world's best-known and best-selling soft drink.

slump. By the mid-1920s, cotton production was less than half of its pre–World War I level. The result was much hardship for the hundreds of thousands of Georgians—white and African-American alike—who depended on cotton for their livelihood.

The Great Depression and World War II

In 1929, the New York Stock Exchange crashed. Within two years, the entire United States was plunged into an economic depression. This nationwide slump further lowered cotton prices and increased the misery felt by Georgia's poorest citizens. Thousands of Georgians moved off their land. Many of them left the state altogether, heading to the cities of the North to search, usually unsuccessfully, for employment.

The state steadily lost population in the early 1930s as Georgians moved to other states in search of work. Those who remained struggled to make ends meet any way they could. For many, this meant long hours of backbreaking, low-wage work in the state's many textile mills.

Georgia's mills had been turning cotton into cloth since before the Civil War, but the state's textile industry greatly expanded in the first decades of the 20th century. Textile manufacturers—mostly large companies based in the North—built mills in Georgia and other Southern states, where labor and transportation costs were low and labor unions were weak.

In 1934, strikes swept some of Georgia's textile mills. Governor Eugene Talmadge called out the National Guard to put down the strikes. A hot-tempered and outspoken leader in the tradition of Thomas Watson, Talmadge dominated Georgia politics in the 1930s and 1940s. Drawing his support from the state's businessmen and small farmers, he denounced labor unions as "communistic" and opposed any kind of civil rights for the African Americans of Georgia.

Talmadge was also a foe of President Franklin Delano Roosevelt, whose New Deal programs helped ease the Depression for many Americans. Talmadge called Roosevelt's New Deal "plain foolishness," and the president's programs made little headway in Georgia until Talmadge was voted out of office in 1936. (Georgians returned him to the governor's mansion in Atlanta four years later.)

With the coming of World War II, Georgia's economy revived, as did the nation's. Government orders for defense goods poured into the state's mills, factories, and shipyards, and the demand for cotton and food crops shot up as well. The first stirrings of Georgia's postwar high-tech industry came at this time, too, in the form of

This Greene County textile mill (above) was photographed in 1941, when a flood of government orders brought Georgia's Depression-ravaged economy back to life—and seven years after striking mill workers faced bullets and clubs during bloody strikes.

Eugene Talmadge (1884–1946) (right) was a teacher, lawyer, and mule salesman before entering politics as state commissioner of agriculture. He served two terms as governor in the 1930s and another in the early 1940s. Again elected governor in 1946, he died before he could take office. His son Herman served as Georgia's governor and in the U.S. Senate.

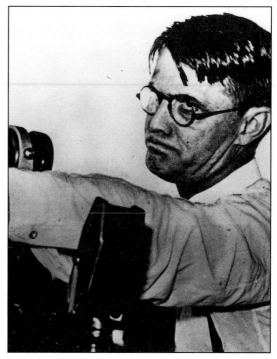

Bell Aircraft, which set up a big plant in Marietta.

Thanks to its warm climate, which allowed year-round training of troops and good flying conditions, Georgia became home to a number of military bases. Some, like the army's Fort Benning near Columbus, were World War I establishments expanded to meet the needs of the new conflict. Others, including Hunter Field air base outside Savannah, sprang up almost overnight.

The state had 320,000 men and women in uniform during the four years of war—that is almost one out of every ten Georgians. Nearly 7,000 of them lost their lives defending their country.

Many Georgians felt a special kinship to President Franklin Roosevelt, who remained in office during World War II. Roosevelt had been stricken by polio in 1921, and afterward passed several long periods at the resort at Warm Springs, Georgia, where the waters helped him. Roosevelt in turn helped make Warm Springs an important rehabilitation center for polio sufferers. As president he often returned to Warm Springs for vacations.

It was at the Little White House at Warm Springs that Roosevelt suffered a fatal stroke on April 12, 1945. When the train bearing his body left Warm Springs for Washington, thousands of tearful Georgians lined the railroad tracks.

President Franklin Delano Roosevelt sat for this portrait at Warm Springs in the days before he died there on April 12, 1945. The painting, by Elizabeth Shoumatoff, was never completed.

The Struggle for Civil Rights

The Second World War transformed 20th-century Georgia, just as the Revolutionary War and the Civil War had transformed the state in the 18th and 19th centuries.

The war sent Georgia's industrial expansion, which had begun in the late 1800s, into high gear. That expansion continued after peace came in 1945 and the state's plants and factories switched to making goods for the booming civilian market. By 1950, more Georgians worked in factories than on farms for the first time in the state's history.

The postwar industrial boom helped break up the old sharecropping system, already in decline since the boll weevil crisis. It also increased the movement of people from the countryside to Georgia's growing cities.

This was especially true for Georgia's African Americans. From 1940 onward, thousands of African Americans left the state to take jobs in the North. The census of 1950 found that Georgia's African-American population had fallen from 40 percent of the total at the turn of the century to about 30 percent in 1950.

African Americans who remained in Georgia moved by the hundreds of thousands from country to cities. Before World War II, most African-American Georgians lived on farms. Within two decades of the war's end, almost all lived in urban areas.

Whether in the country or city, however, Georgia's African Americans still felt the injustice of the South's long-standing system of segregation—a system that denied them educational and job opportunities and kept them out of the mainstream of Georgia society.

The post–World War II years saw the rise of a movement that was aimed at guaranteeing civil and political rights to African Americans and ending Jim Crow, as the segregation system was nicknamed.

The first stirrings of the civil rights movement in Georgia came toward the end of World War II. In 1944, fifty African-American students in Savannah refused to give up their seats to white passengers on one of the city's segregated buses. A year later, African Americans—many of them World War II veterans—marched in Atlanta to demand desegregation of the city's all-white police force.

In a 1954 Supreme Court case—*Brown v. Board of Education of Topeka, Kansas*—segregation in public schools was ruled unconstitutional. Despite the court's demand that Southern states integrate their school systems "with all deliberate speed," Georgia's legislature acted with deliberate slowness. It wasn't until 1961 that public-school desegregation began at all. In the late 1960s, the federal government ordered Georgia to speed up the process.

The greatest figure of the civil rights movement, Martin Luther King, Jr., was a native Georgian. After leading a successful boycott of the segregated bus system in Montgomery, Alabama, King returned to his home town of Atlanta in 1960 to become pastor of the city's Ebenezer Baptist Church.

From his pulpit at Ebenezer, and in countless speeches, marches, and demonstrations, King called on Americans to fight prejudice and segregation through nonviolent protest. Inspired by King's message, whites and African Americans in Georgia and other states began a campaign of sit in demonstrations aimed at ending segregation in restaurants, theaters, buses, and other public places. In 1960, major sit-in protests in Atlanta and Savannah finally cracked the wall of segregation that had kept whites

Martin Luther King, Jr. (1929–68) is shown here speaking to an audience at Harvard University. Following his assassination, King's body was returned to Atlanta, where a crowd of 200,000 people stood by as a mule-drawn wagon bore the slain leader's body to its final resting place.

and African Americans in separate and unequal societies.

This civil rights movement met with opposition and sometimes violence from Georgian whites. Many felt that federal support for civil rights violated the rights of state governments. In Georgia, opposition to civil rights was led by Lester Maddox, an Atlanta restaurant owner who was elected governor in 1966.

But Maddox and his supporters couldn't stem the civil rights tide. In 1963, King led 500,000 people on a march to Washington. From the steps of the Lincoln Memorial, King gave a stirring speech, one that continues to inspire people around the world: "I have a dream," it began, ". . . that one day on the red hills of Georgia sons of former slaves and sons of former slaveowners will be able to sit down at the table of brotherhood."

In 1964 and 1965, major federal laws guaranteed basic civil and political rights to African Americans. Over the next few years, the barriers between African Americans and whites began to fall in Georgia and other Southern states.

King, however, would not live to see his dream become a reality. He was killed by an assassin's bullet in Memphis, Tennessee, in 1968. Today, Atlanta's Martin Luther King, Jr. Center for Non-Violent Social Change honors his achievement and continues his work.

Named communications director of the Student Nonviolent Coordinating Committee in 1960, Julian Bond (b. 1940) was later one of Georgia's first African Americans to hold elective office after Reconstruction. He served as a state legislator from 1965 to 1975, when he was elected to Georgia's senate.

Busy Decades of Growth

"South of the North, yet North of the South, lies the city of a hundred hills, peering out of the shadows of the past into the promise of the future." This is how the great African-American scholar W.E.B. DuBois described the Atlanta of 1903. His words also apply to the Atlanta of the post–World War II decades.

Atlanta grew spectacularly after World War II. The city greatly increased in size in 1952, when several outlying counties were incorporated into the city itself. The movement of Georgians from the countryside to the cities led to a population boom in Atlanta and provided plenty of labor for Atlanta's thriving industries. By the 1960s, Atlanta was the financial, industrial, and economic capital not only of Georgia but of the entire South.

Much of this growth came from the efforts of far-seeing Atlantans like Ivan Allen, Jr., who launched the "Forward Atlanta" campaign shortly before his election as mayor in 1961. The campaign, aimed at bringing even more businesses to the city, was a success: Between 1960 and 1968, $1 billion worth of new buildings rose skyward in Atlanta.

Although Atlanta saw plenty of racial tension during the height of the civil rights movement, the city was spared much of the violence that accompanied desegregation in other Southern cities. This was due, in part, to the leadership of Allen and his predecessor as mayor, William Hartsfield, who liked to say that Atlanta was "a city too busy to hate." An important sign of racial progress in Georgia came in 1973, when Maynard Jackson took office as Atlanta's first African-American mayor. (By this time, about half of Atlanta's residents were African Americans.)

Atlanta's growth continued during Jackson's eight years in office, with the city and its suburbs more than doubling in area and population. The Peachtree Center mall complex, pride of Atlanta, opened in the mid-1970s.

In fact, the 1970s was a decade of growth for the whole state. Between 1970 and 1980, Georgia gained almost 875,000 new residents—an annual growth rate of almost 2 percent, or nearly twice the national average. During these years, Georgia also benefited from the movement of businesses from the Rust Belt states of the Northeast to the Sun Belt states of the South and Southwest. Also, many African Americans who had left Georgia years before returned in the 1970s when job and educational

Elected vice mayor of Atlanta in 1969, Maynard Jackson (b. 1938) (top) became the city's first African-American mayor four years later. He remained in office until 1982, when he was succeeded by Andrew Young, a veteran of the civil rights movement and former United States ambassador to the United Nations.

This cafe (right) is inside the Peachtree Center, the showpiece of downtown Atlanta. The striking architecture and artwork of the complex can be seen in the photograph.

opportunities opened up as segregation ended.

Georgia's governor from 1971 to 1975 was James Earl Carter, known to all as Jimmy, a former naval officer and peanut farmer from the town of Plains. Carter took office at a time when many Georgians were still divided over civil rights issues. In his inaugural address he left no doubt where he stood, saying, "The time for racial discrimination is over."

Although little-known on the national political scene, Carter decided to run for president after leaving the governor's mansion. He captured the Democratic nomination and defeated incumbent Republican Gerald Ford in the election of 1976 to become the first Georgian ever in the White House.

As president, Carter gained a reputation for honesty and achieved some important foreign policy victories, including the 1977 Camp David peace agreement between Israel and Egypt. However, his term also saw rising energy prices, a sluggish national economy, and the seizure of American hostages in Iran. Carter was defeated in his reelection bid in 1980.

After leaving the White House, Carter became one of America's most active and energetic ex-presidents. He and his wife, Rosalynn, became involved in many social causes, and Carter undertook peace missions to trouble spots such as Haiti and Bosnia.

Jimmy Carter (b. 1924) wears his trademark smile in his official presidential photograph. Carter, president from 1977–1981, was the first Georgian to occupy the White House.

The State of Georgia Today

By the mid-1980s, Georgia's population had passed the 6-million mark. By the early 1990s, that figure was approaching 7 million.

Today, seven out of ten Georgians live in towns and cities—and four of ten live in Atlanta or its ever-expanding ring of suburbs. The census of 1990 showed that the Atlanta metropolitan area was the twelfth-largest in the United States, with almost 3 million residents. The Crossroads of the South since before the Civil War, Atlanta remains a vital transportation hub in the jet age. Hartsfield International Airport, which opened in 1980, was the nation's fourth-busiest air terminal in 1993.

Atlanta is a major communications center, too, thanks to cable-TV executive Ted Turner. In 1970, Turner purchased his first TV station in Atlanta, and over the next twenty-five years his media empire expanded to include TBS, TNT, CNN Headline News, and the Cartoon Network. Turner also owns two of the city's professional sports teams, the Atlanta Braves (baseball) and the Atlanta Hawks (basketball).

Despite Georgia's rapid industrial growth in the second half of the 20th century, agriculture remains important to the state. Timber and wood products are a major export, and much of the state's old cotton lands have been replanted with pines and other trees. Fruit crops, especially pecans and peanuts, also make an important contribution to the state's economy.

Most of Georgia's rural areas, however, haven't matched the state's cities in population growth and economic prosperity. Some people now speak of two Georgias—the prosperous cities like Atlanta, Macon, Savannah, and Augusta, and the poorer rural counties. The situation in the Georgia countryside worsened in 1988, when a period of drought parched croplands across the state.

Like all Americans, Georgians have had to cope with the effects of industrial and population growth on the environment and on natural resources. In 1964, the state government set up its first environmental agency, the Water Control Board, to halt the effects of pollution on the state's waterways. In the 1970s, Georgia combined the Water Control Board with other environmental agencies to form the Environmental Protection Division. One of the division's major efforts in recent years has been to clean up the Savannah River, where pollution from industry and sewage reached dangerous levels.

The Atlanta skyline shines at night in this 1994 photograph. More than 1,200 international businesses now operate in Atlanta: This fact—plus the 1996 Olympic Games—has made Atlanta not only Georgia's biggest city and capital but a major international city as well.

Ted Turner (b. 1938) transformed the telecommunications industry with his cable-TV ventures. Millions of people around the world rely on Turner's Cable News Network (CNN)—which broadcasts from CNN Center in downtown Atlanta—for up-to-the-minute news.

Problems remain, as well, for Georgia's African Americans, despite their great political and economic strides in recent decades. Areas of high unemployment, crime, and poverty plague African-American communities even in prosperous cities like Atlanta. And while segregation is now a thing of the past, discrimination against African Americans is not. In 1987, for example, the Ku Klux Klan and other white supremacist groups marched in rural Forsyth County in an effort to keep African-American families from moving into the area.

Still, the story of modern Georgia is a story of remarkable and enduring success. Little more than half a century ago, Georgia was a mostly rural, agricultural state that lagged behind much of the nation in literacy, prosperity, and public health. Many of Georgia's citizens were denied basic rights and opportunities because of their race.

Today, Georgia is the South's leader in commerce, industry, transportation, and other important areas, and it boasts one of the nation's fastest-growing and most dynamic cities—Atlanta. Many of the barriers that kept Georgia's African Americans from their rightful place as citizens have finally fallen.

Georgians of all races, in rural counties and cities alike, rejoiced in 1990 when the International Olympic Committee announced that Atlanta

The best-known Georgian on the national political scene today is Republican Newt Gingrich (b. 1943). First elected to Congress in 1978, Gingrich became Speaker of the House of Representatives in January 1995.

would host the 1996 Summer Olympic Games. By the end of 1995, Atlantans were busily gearing up for the 700,000 spectators expected to come to the games in the summer of 1996.

When the Olympic Torch was lit, the eyes of the world were focused on a city—and a state—whose citizens look to the future with hope and pride.

Land area:

58,876 square miles, of which 679 are inland water. Twenty-first largest state.

Major rivers:

The Altamaha River; the Chattahoochee River; the Etowah River; the Flint River; the Ocmulgee River; the Oconee River; the Ogeechee River; the St. Marys River; the Satilla River; the Savannah River; the Tallulah River.

Highest point:

Brasstown Bald Mountain, 4,784 ft.

Major bodies of water:

Allatoona Lake; Clarks Hill Lake; Hartwell Lake; Lake Oconee; Lake Seminole; Lake Sidney Lanier; Lake Sinclair; Walter F. George Reservoir.

Climate:

Average January temperature: 49° F
Average July temperature: 80° F

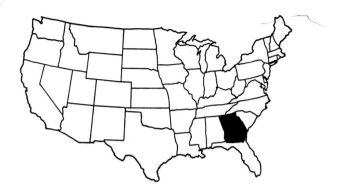

Population: 6,917,140 (1993)
Rank: 11th
    1900: 2,216,331
    1820: 340,989

Population of major cities (1990):

Atlanta	393,929
Columbus	178,681
Savannah	137,812
Macon	107,365
Albany	78,804
Roswell	47,986
Athens	45,734
Augusta	44,707

Ethnic breakdown by percentage (1993):

White	71.0%
African American	27.0%
Hispanic	1.7%
Other	0.3%

Economy:
Manufacturing (especially textile processing), timber products (lumber, paper products, furniture), food processing (especially fruit and seafood), agriculture (peanuts, cotton, soybeans, pecans, tobacco), poultry and cattle, telecommunications.

State Government:
Legislature: The General Assembly consists of a 56-member senate and a 180-member house of representatives. Members of both houses are elected to two-year terms.

Governor: The governor heads the executive branch of the state government and is elected for a four-year term but for no more than two consecutive terms.

Courts: Georgia has a three-level court system, with supreme, appellate, and trial courts. Supreme and appellate court judges are elected by the voters; some judges in the lower courts are elected, while others are appointed by the governor.

State Capital: Atlanta.

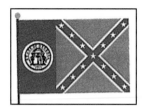

State Flag

Georgia's state flag features the state seal on a blue background plus the stars-and-bars of the Confederate battle flag. Adopted in 1956, the flag has been a source of controversy because of its connection with the Confederacy.

State Seal

Adopted in 1799, the state seal features an arch symbolizing the state constitution. The arch is supported by three columns representing elements of the state motto. Georgia's signing of the Declaration of Independence is commemorated by the figure of a Patriot and the date 1776.

State Motto

"Wisdom, Justice, Moderation."

State Nickname

Georgia is known by several unofficial nicknames, including the "Peach State" and "Empire State of the South" (from its size and economic importance).

Places

Alexander H. Stephens State Historic Park, Crawfordville

Amicalola Falls State Park, Dawsonville

Andersonville National Historic Site, Andersonville

Black Rock Mountain State Park, Clayton

Brasstown Bald Mountain, Blairsville

Callaway Plantation, Washington

Chehaw Wild Animal Park, Albany

Chickamauga and Chattanooga National Military Park, U.S. RT 27

Crawford W. Long Museum, Jefferson

Crisson's Gold Mines, Dahlonega

Elijah Clark State Park, Lincolnton

Etowah Indian Mounds, Cartersville

Fort Frederica, St. Simons Island

Fort Pulaski National Monument, Savannah

Georgia Agrirama, Tifton

Georgia Veterans' Memorial State Park, Cordele

Harriet Tubman Museum, Macon

Jefferson-Davis Memorial Park, Ocilla

Jekyll Island Club Historical District, Jekyll Island

to See

Juliette Gordon Low Birthplace, Savannah

Kennesaw Mountain National Battlefield Park, Kennesaw

Kolomoki Mounds State Park, Blakely

Martin Luther King, Jr. Center for Nonviolent Social Change, Atlanta

Midway Church & Museum, Midway

National Infantry Museum, Fort Benning

New Echota, Calhoun

Ocmulgee National Monument & Museum, Macon

Okefenokee Swamp Park, Waycross

Old Market House, Louisville

Old State Capitol Museum, Milledgeville

Robert W. Woodruff Arts Center, Atlanta

Roosevelt's Little White House Historic Site, Warm Springs

Savannah Historic District, Savannah

Stately Oaks Plantation Home, Jonesboro

Stone Mountain Park, Stone Mountain

Tallulah Gorge, Tallulah Falls

Tybee Island Lighthouse, Tybee Island

Westville Village, Lumpkin

Woodrow Wilson Boyhood Home Augusta

State Flower

The white-petalled Cherokee rose was named Georgia's "floral symbol" in 1916. According to legend, the flower was brought to Georgia by the Cherokee wife of a Seminole warrior. Georgia also has an official state wildflower—the azalea.

State Bird

Georgia's state bird, the brown thrasher, is about eleven inches long and has a reddish-brown and white tail. The bird tosses aside leaves with its beak while searching for food, hence the name "thrasher."

State Tree

The live oak (*Quercus virginiana*), Georgia's state tree, is a low tree with wide spreading branches. Its name comes from the Spanish moss that grows on its limbs.

Georgia History

1539-40 Spanish explorer Hernando de Soto crosses Georgia on his journey through southeastern North America

1732 General James Oglethorpe establishes Georgia as a colony; Savannah is settled the next year

1742 Battle of Bloody Marsh: Oglethorpe's forces defeat the Spanish on St. Simons Island

1752 Georgia becomes a royal colony

1776 Three delegates from Georgia sign the Declaration of Independence

1778 British forces capture Savannah and gain control of most of Georgia until 1782

1788 Georgia ratifies the Constitution—the fourth state to do so

1792 Eli Whitney develops the cotton gin at the Greene Plantation outside Savannah

1826 The Creeks give up their Georgia homelands

1838 The Trail of Tears: Georgia's Cherokees are forced to leave the state

1845 The town of Terminus, at the junction of several railroads, is renamed Atlanta

1861 Georgia secedes from the Union and joins the Confederacy

1863 Union forces are defeated in the bloody Battle of Chickamauga

American

1492 Christopher Columbus reaches America

1607 Jamestown (Virginia) founded by English colonists

1620 *Mayflower* arrives at Plymouth (Massachusetts)

1754-63 French and Indian War

1765 Parliament passes Stamp Act

1775-83 Revolutionary War

1776 Signing of the Declaration of Independence

1788-90 First congressional elections

1791 Bill of Rights added to U.S. Consitution

1803 Louisiana Purchase

1812-14 War of 1812

1820 Missouri Compromise

1836 Battle of the Alamo (Texas)

1846-48 Mexican-American War

1849 California Gold Rush

1860 South Carolina secedes from Union

1861-65 Civil War

1862 Lincoln signs Homestead Act

1863 Emancipation Proclamation

1865 President Lincoln assassinated (April 14)

1865-77 Reconstruction in the South

1866 Civil Rights bill passed

1881 President James Garfield shot (July 2)

History

1896 First Ford automobile is made

1898-99 Spanish-American War

1901 President William McKinley is shot (Sept. 6)

1917 U.S. enters World War I

1922 Nineteenth Amendment passed, giving women the vote

1929 U.S. stock market crash; Great Depression begins

1933 Franklin D. Roosevelt becomes president; begins New Deal

1941 Japanese attack Pearl Harbor (Dec. 7); U.S. enters World War II

1945 U.S. drops atomic bomb on Hiroshima and Nagasaki; Japan surrenders, ending World War II

1963 President Kennedy assassinated (November 22)

1964 Civil Rights Act passed

1965-73 Vietnam War

1968 Martin Luther King, Jr., shot in Memphis (April 4)

1974 President Richard Nixon resigns because of Watergate scandal

1978-81 Hostage crisis in Iran: 52 Americans held captive for 444 days

1989 End of U.S.-Soviet cold war

1991 U.S enters the Gulf War

1995 Terrorists bomb a federal building in Oklahoma City

Georgia History

1864 Union general William Tecumseh Sherman captures Atlanta and marches across the state to Savannah

1865 Confederate president Jefferson Davis is captured near Irwinville

1870 Georgia is re-admitted to the Union

1877 Atlanta becomes Georgia's permanent state capital

1886 Atlanta pharmacist John Pemberton invents Coca-Cola

1912 Juliette Gordon Low of Savannah founds the Girl Scouts of America

1934 Textile-mill strikes hit the Depression-ravaged state

1937 Margaret Mitchell of Atlanta wins the Pulitzer Prize for her Civil War novel *Gone With The Wind*

1945 President Franklin D. Roosevelt dies at the "Little White House" in Warm Springs

1973 Maynard Jackson, Jr., is elected mayor of Atlanta, becoming the first African-America mayor of a major Southern city

1976 Jimmy Carter of Plains becomes the nation's thirty-ninth president

1994 Georgian Newt Gingrich becomes speaker of the House of Representatives

1996 The Summer Olympic Games open in Atlanta

James Oglethorpe (1696–1785) In 1732, this English soldier and member of parliament obtained a charter from King George II to found the colony that eventually became the state of Georgia. From 1733 to 1743, Oglethorpe governed and defended the colony, which he hoped would provide a refuge for Britain's poorer citizens.

Nathanael Greene (1742–86) One of the ablest commanders in the Revolutionary War, Greene, born in Rhode Island, led the Patriot forces in the South during the final stage of the conflict. After independence was won, he retired to a Georgia plantation, Mulberry Grove, where the cotton gin was later invented.

Nathanael Greene

Sequoya (c. 1760–1843) Also known as George Guess, this Cherokee silversmith turned his brilliant mind to the task of creating a written version of the Cherokee language. By 1821, he had developed an alphabet to represent Cherokee speech and the first Cherokee language newspaper followed a few years later.

Robert Augustus Toombs (1810–85) One of the most outspoken advocates of slavery and states' rights, Toombs served in the House of Representatives (1845–53) and the Senate (1853–61). In 1861, he was named the Confederacy's secretary of state, a post he left to serve as a Confederate general.

Joel Chandler Harris (1848–1908) A keen student of Georgia folklore, Harris wrote stories inspired by the tales of Georgia's African Americans. Many of his works, including the famous Uncle Remus series, first appeared in the Atlanta *Constitution* newspaper.

Asa Griggs Candler (1851–1929) In 1887, Candler bought the formula for a carbonated drink called Coca-Cola, which another Atlanta pharmacist, John Pemberton, had invented the year before. Through shrewd marketing, Candler made Coca-Cola a household name around the world and built a huge business empire.

Thomas Edward Watson (1856–1922) Known as "Pa" Watson, this fiery politician rose to power in Georgia as a Populist at the turn of the century. Watson served in the House of Representatives (1891–93) and the Senate (1921–22) and is best remembered today for sponsoring the bill providing free mail delivery to all Americans in rural areas.

Juliette Gordon Low (1860–1927) This Savannah-born artist founded the Girl Scouts of America in 1913. She served as the organization's president until 1920.

Margaret Mitchell (1900–49) Born into a prosperous Atlanta family, Mitchell worked as a reporter before publishing her best-selling Civil War novel, *Gone With the Wind*, in 1936. The book was followed three years later by a movie version.

Bobby Jones

Bobby Jones (1902–71)

Considered by some to be the greatest golfer of all time, Atlanta-born Robert Tyre Jones, Jr., stunned the golf world in 1930 by winning every major tournament in a single year.

Erskine Caldwell (1903–87)

This White Oak–born writer shot to national fame with *Tobacco Road* (1932), a novel about a sharecropper family. For a time, Caldwell was one of America's best-known and critically praised writers.

Jackie Robinson (1919–72)

Jack Roosevelt Robinson joined the Brooklyn Dodgers in 1947, becoming the first African American to play in the major leagues, and ending segregation in professional baseball. The Cairo-born hitter's career included six pennants and one world series victory.

Jimmy Carter (b. 1924)

Son of a Plains peanut farmer, Carter was elected governor of Georgia in 1971. Five years later, he defeated Republican Gerald Ford for the presidency. Events like the energy crisis of the late 1970s and the Iran hostage crisis (1979–81) marred his administration and in 1980 he was defeated for reelection by Ronald Reagan. After leaving office, Carter devoted his time to social work and international relations.

Martin Luther King, Jr. (1929–68)

This Atlanta-born Baptist minister was the greatest figure of the civil-rights movement of the 1950s and 1960s. His insistence on nonviolent protest led to passage of the Civil Rights Act of 1964 and the Voting Rights Act of 1964. That year, King received the Nobel Prize for Peace. He was assassinated in Memphis, Tennessee in 1968.

Andrew Young, Jr. (b. 1932)

A close associate of Dr. Martin Luther King, Jr., Young was director of the Southern Christian Leadership Conference (SCLC). Young served as mayor of Atlanta from 1982 to 1989 and in 1990 made a failed bid for governor.

Ted Turner (b. 1938)

Turner revolutionized television entertainment and information with his Turner Broadcasting Network (TBN) and Cable News Network (CNN). He is also famous for his ownership of the Atlanta Braves and the Atlanta Hawks. Turner is married to the actress Jane Fonda.

Maynard H. Jackson, Jr. (b. 1938)

Jackson made history in 1973 when he was elected mayor of Atlanta—the first African-American mayor of a large Southern city. A popular mayor, Jackson left office in 1982 because the law forbids more than two consecutive terms. He was again elected mayor in 1989.

Newt Gingrich (b. 1943)

Born in Pennsylvania, Gingrich came to Georgia in the early 1960s. He was elected to Congress in 1978, and in 1994, when the Republican Party won a majority in Congress, Gingrich became speaker of the House of Representatives.

Pictures in this volume:

Dover: 9 (left), 38

Georgia Department of Tourism: 52 (top)

John Portman and Associates: 49 (bottom)

Library of Congress: 10-11, 12, 13, 14, 15, 16, 18, 19 (both), 20, 21, 22, 23, 24, 25, 26-27, 28, 30, 31, 32, 34, 37 (top), 40 (both), 43 (top), 44, 46, 60

McClung Museum, U. Tennessee: 9 (right)

MPI Archives: 7, 29, 41

National Archives: 49 (top), 61

National Park Service: 17

New York Public Library: 35, 37 (bottom), 47

Turner Broadcasting System, Inc.: 52 (bottom)

United States Congress: 53

University of Georgia Library: 39, 43 (bottom)

White House: 50

About the author:

Charles A. Wills is a writer, editor, and consultant specializing in American history. He has written, edited, or contributed to more than thirty books, including many volumes in The Millbrook Press's *American Albums from the Collections of the Library of Congress* series. Wills lives in Dutchess County, New York.

Suggested reading:

Fradin, Dennis B., *Georgia In Words and Pictures*, Chicago: The Children's Press, 1981

—, *The Georgia Colony*, Chicago: The Children's Press, 1990

Hepburn, Lawrence, *The Georgia History Book*, Athens, GA: University of Georgia Press, 1982

Mitchell, Margaret, *Gone With the Wind*, New York: Avon, 1974

Rogers, Jan Faulk, *Georgia: Home of President Jimmy Carter*, Chicago: The Children's Press, 1978

Snow, Pegeen, *Atlanta: A Downtown America Book*, Minneapolis: Dillon Press, 1988

Wingo, W. Bruce, *Adventures In Georgia*, Stone Mountain, GA.: Linton Day, 1989

For more information contact:

Georgia Department of Industry Trade and Tourism
P.O. Box 1776
Atlanta, GA 30301-1776
(404)656-3590

Georgia State Department of Archives and History
330 Capitol Avenue., SE
Atlanta, GA 30334
(404) 656-2350

Page numbers in *italics* indicate illustrations